IN THE PRESENCE OF THE SUN

✷ *In the Presence of the Sun*

STORIES AND POEMS, 1961–1991

N. SCOTT MOMADAY
Illustrations by N. SCOTT MOMADAY

UNIVERSITY OF NEW MEXICO • ALBUQUERQUE

13 12 11 10 09   1 2 3 4 5

LIBRARY OF CONGRESS CATALOGING-IN-PUBLICATION DATA

Momaday, N. Scott, 1934–

In the presence of the sun : stories and poems, 1961–1991 /

  N. Scott Momaday.

  p. cm.

  ISBN 978-0-8263-4816-6 (pbk. : alk. paper)

1. Indians of North America—Literary collections. I. Title.

PS3563.O4715 2009

  813´54—dc22

            2009039089

NOTE: Part III of this volume was originally published in a signed
and limited edition by the Rydal Press, Santa Fe, New Mexico. Other
previously published material has appeared in the following: *The Santa Fe
New Mexican* (1970–72); *The Stanford Magazine* (Spring–Summer, 1975);
Carriers of the Dream Wheel, Duane Niatum, ed., Harper & Row (1975);
and *The Gourd Dancer*, by N. Scott Momaday, Harper and Row (1976).

To my daughters

Contents

THE STRANGE AND TRUE STORY OF
MY LIFE WITH BILLY THE KID

IN THE PRESENCE OF THE SUN:
A GATHERING OF SHIELDS

NEW POEMS

List of Illustrations

Acknowledgments

Those to whom I am indebted in one way or another for the realization of this work are many, indeed more than I know. Here are names that come immediately to mind: Natachee Scott Momaday, Alfred Morris Momaday, Yvor Winters, Janet Lewis, Leonard Baskin, Fray Angelico Chavez, Helen Houghton, Olga Sergeevna Akhmanova, Bobby Jack Nelson, Bernard Pomerance, William Jay Smith, and Regina Heitzer-Momaday. To these I pay my best thanks. I should like also to thank Clark Kimball, whose Rydal Press edition of *In the Presence of the Sun: A Gathering of Shields*, which comprises the third part of this trade edition, is a singular example of the bookmaker's art; Bob Weil, my editor at St. Martin's Press, whose friendship, advice, and encouragement have kept me to the task; Barbara Andrews and Stephanie Schwartz of St. Martin's, whose enthusiasm and efforts have been greatly appreciated; and Arlene LewAllen, who for several years now has steadily seen to the development of my painting and printmaking.

And I am especially grateful to Barbara Gregg Glenn for being, among other things, a reader of absolute attention and nearly perfect perception.

N.S.M.

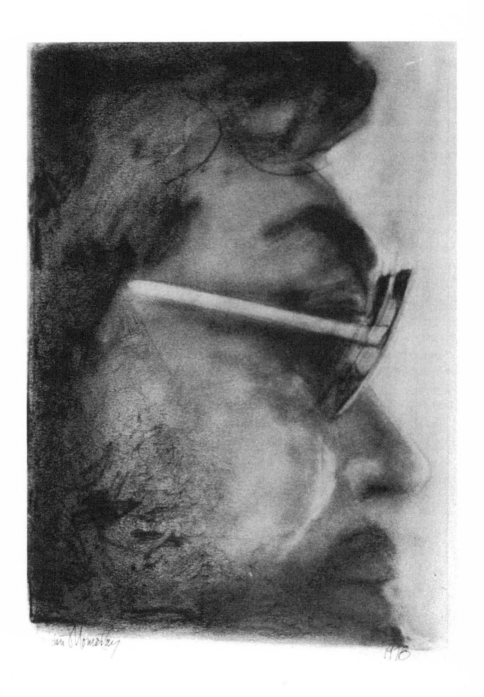

Preface

The poems in this collection were written over a period of thirty years, the drawings drawn over something less than twenty. In the same span I have written a good many other things, novels, essays, an autobiographical narrative, a play. My drawings, paintings, and prints have been exhibited in galleries and museums in this country and abroad. I have been, from the time I was in my twenties, a productive artist, not a prolific one as I think of it, but neither a straggler. Deadlines are useful but in some sense alien to my work. I believe that poems and paintings are made as they are made. I like to work in different forms. When I knew what it was to write a poem, I wanted to know what it was to write a novel, then a travel piece, then a film script, then a play. When I had found my way with charcoal and graphite, I went to watercolor and acrylics, to oils, to printmaking. I was and remain a patient student. With every attempt to write a line or draw an image I have learned something. I have tried to keep my mind alive for the sake of learning, which is to say for its own sake. That is my reason for doing what I do and for being who I am.

Thirty years is a long time or not, depending upon your point of view. My point of view is a plateau from which I view the world in my fifty-seventh year. Below I can see, in the very far distance, the dim figures of my ancestors, entering upon this continent thirty thousand years ago. Closer I can see Columbus touching upon the island he named San Salvador, and closer and closer by degrees, such things as the founding of Harvard College and the publication of the first book on the first printing press in New England, the signing of the Declaration of Independence, the Battle of Gettysburg, the last Kiowa Sun Dance in 1887, the great influenza epidemic of 1918 in which my maternal grandmother died, the great World Wars (I was born between them), the civil rights movement, the assassinations of John and Robert Kennedy and of Martin Luther King, the footprints of man on the moon, the assault of AIDS upon the human race, the collapse of the Soviet Union, and a growing awareness, as yet vague, that human beings, for all their assumed superiority over the plants and animals of the earth, have inflicted wounds upon the environment that are surely much more serious than we have realized, that may indeed be mortal. As a poet, a painter, and a man I care about these things. My life is involved in them.

I have been called "the man made of words," a phrase that I myself coined some years ago in connection with a Kiowa folktale. It is an identity that pleases me. In a sense, a real sense, my life has been composed of words. Reading and writing, talking, telling stories, listening, remembering, and thinking (someone has said that thinking is talking to oneself) have been the cornerstones of my existence. Words inform the element in which I live my daily life.

Poetry is a very old and elemental expression, as venerable as song and prayer. In various times and languages we have tried to elevate it to our current notions of formality and eloquence. And we have succeeded, for language, by its nature, allows us to do so. But poetry remains elemental. In poetry we address ourselves really, without pretension or deceit, without the intervention of interest. At its best, poetry is an act of disinterested generosity. The poet gives his words to the world in the appropriate expression of his spirit. It belongs to none in particular and to everyone in general. "This is my letter to the world," Emily Dickinson wrote. It is a viable definition of poetry.

From the time I could first function in language, I have been in love with words. How I gloried to hear my father tell the old Kiowa stories, which existed only at the level of the human voice. And how I loved my mother to invent stories in which I played the principal part. In my earliest years I lived in a home that was informed by the imagination, by the telling of stories and the celebration of language. Not only that, but I lived on several American Indian reservations in those days. I fell in love with Tanoan and Athabascan and Spanish and English words. Even now I can hear old people conversing in *Diné bizaad*, the Navajo language, and I am thrilled; I am transported to a time when I was a child at Chinle and heard wonderful words echoing on the cliffs of Canyon de Chelly. When I attend the Gourd Dance at

Carnegie, Oklahoma, in July, the Kiowa language buoys me up in my spirit, and my being is defined in ancestral voices.

Words are names. To write a poem is to practice a naming ceremony.

> These figures moving in my rhyme,
> Who are they? Death, and Death's dog, time.

And to confer a name is to confer being. We perceive existence by means of words and names. To this or that vague, potential thing I will give a name, and it will exist thereafter, and its existence will be clearly perceived. The name enables me to see it. I can call it by its name, and I can see it for what it is.

The poet says, Here, let me show you something. That is, let me help you to see something as you have not seen it before.

And so says the painter. My father was a painter, and I watched him paint as I was growing up. He belonged to that tradition of Plains Indian art which proceeds from rock paintings to hide paintings to ledgerbook drawings to modern art, so called. He was in line with Zo-tom and the Kiowa Five and Black Bear Bosin. His work was bright and two-dimensional, rich in detail. As he matured his work became mythical and abstract, moored to story and visions. His work became steadily more powerful. His last paintings were his best paintings.

I observed him at work. I learned to see the wonderful things in his mind's eye, how they were translated into images on the picture plane.

In 1974 I accepted an invitation to teach at Moscow State University, and I lived in Moscow, in what was then the U.S.S.R., for six months. It was an experience, a high point in my life. I had much more time to myself than I thought I would, and I spent many, many hours riding the trains and walking the streets with the Muscovites. Richard Nixon fell from power and Aleksandr Solzhenitsyn was expelled from his homeland in those days. Pretty girls asked me to secure banned books for them, and their parents prepared banquets for me.

Something about that time and place made for a surge in me, a kind of creative explosion. I wrote numerous poems, some on the landscapes of my native Southwest, urged, I believe, by an acute homesickness. And I began to sketch. Drawing became suddenly very important to me, and I haunted museums and galleries and looked into as many Russian sketchbooks as I could find. When I came out of the Soviet Union I brought with me a new way of seeing and a commitment to record it. I moved from charcoal to paint, from black and white to color, from paper to canvas, and back again. In Europe I discovered painters who truly inspired me: Emil Nolde, Francis Bacon, Pablo Picasso (whose work I thought I knew but did not), Georg Baselitz.

I had my first show in 1979, at the University of North Dakota Art Galleries. As I write this, I am preparing for a show at the Wheelwright Museum in Santa Fe, a retrospective; after nearly two decades of work, it is time. I feel that I have finished the first chapter of life as a painter.

The poems and stories, the drawings here, express my spirit fairly, I believe. If you look closely into these pages, it is possible to catch a glimpse of me in my original being.

N. Scott Momaday
Harvard, 1992

In the Presence of the Sun

STORIES AND POEMS, 1961–1991

✹ SELECTED
POEMS

The Bear

What ruse of vision,
escarping the wall of leaves,
    rending incision
into countless surfaces,

    would cull and color
his somnolence, whose old age
    has outworn valor,
all but the fact of courage?

    Seen, he does not come,
move, but seems forever there,
    dimensionless, dumb,
in the windless noon's hot glare.

    More scarred than others
these years since the trap maimed him,
    pain slants his withers,
drawing up the crooked limb.

    Then he is gone, whole,
without urgency, from sight,
    as buzzards control,
imperceptibly, their flight.

Buteo Regalis

His frailty discrete, the rodent turns, looks.
What sense first warns? The winging is unheard,
Unseen but as distant motion made whole,
Singular, slow, unbroken in its glide.
It veers, and veering, tilts broad-surfaced wings.
Aligned, the span bends to begin the dive
And falls, alternately white and russet,
Angle and curve, gathering momentum.

Comparatives

Sunlit sea,
the drift of fronds,
and banners
of bobbing boats—
the seaside
of any day—
except: this
cold, bright body
of the fish
upon the planks,
the coil and
crescent of flesh
extending
just into death.

Even so,
in the distant,
inland sea,
a shadow runs,
radiant,
rude in the rock:
fossil fish,
fissure of bone
forever.
It is perhaps
the same thing,
an agony
twice perceived.

It is most like
wind on waves—
mere commotion,
mute and mean,
perceptible—
that is all.

Earth and I Gave You Turquoise

Earth and I gave you turquoise
    when you walked singing
We lived laughing in my house
    and told old stories
You grew ill when the owl cried
We will meet on Black Mountain

I will bring corn for planting
    and we will make fire
Children will come to your breast
    You will heal my heart
I speak your name many times
The wild cane remembers you

My young brother's house is filled
    I go there to sing
We have not spoken of you
    but our songs are sad
When Moon Woman goes to you
I will follow her white way

Tonight they dance near Chinle
    by the seven elms
There your loom whispered beauty
    They will eat mutton
and drink coffee till morning
You and I will not be there

I saw a crow by Red Rock
    standing on one leg
It was the black of your hair
    The years are heavy
I will ride the swiftest horse
You will hear the drumming hooves.

Simile

What did we say to each other
that now we are as the deer
who walk in single file
with heads high
with ears forward
with eyes watchful
with hooves always placed on firm ground
in whose limbs there is latent flight

Plainview: 1

There in the hollow of the hills I see,
Eleven magpies stand away from me.

Low light upon the rim; a wind informs
This distance with a gathering of storms

And drifts in silver crescents on the grass,
Configurations that appear, and pass.

There falls a final shadow on the glare,
A stillness on the dark, erratic air.

I do not hear the longer wind that lows
Among the magpies. Silences disclose,

Until no rhythms of unrest remain,
Eleven magpies standing in the plain.

They are illusion—wind and rain revolve—
And they recede in darkness, and dissolve.

Plainview: 2

I saw an old Indian
At Saddle Mountain
He drank and dreamed of drinking
And a blue-black horse

Remember my horse running
  Remember my horse
Remember my horse running
  Remember my horse

Remember my horse wheeling
  Remember my horse
Remember my horse wheeling
  Remember my horse

Remember my horse blowing
  Remember my horse
Remember my horse blowing
  Remember my horse

Remember my horse standing
  Remember my horse
Remember my horse standing
  Remember my horse

Remember my horse hurting
  Remember my horse
Remember my horse hurting
  Remember my horse

Remember my horse falling
  Remember my horse
Remember my horse falling
  Remember my horse

Remember my horse dying
　　Remember my horse
Remember my horse dying
　　Remember my horse

A horse is one thing
An Indian another
An old horse is old
An old Indian is sad

I saw an old Indian
At Saddle Mountain
He drank and dreamed of drinking
And a blue-black horse

Remember my horse running
　　Remember my horse
Remember my horse wheeling
　　Remember my horse
Remember my horse blowing
　　Remember my horse
Remember my horse standing
　　Remember my horse
Remember my horse hurting
　　Remember my horse
Remember my horse falling
　　Remember my horse
Remember my horse dying
　　Remember my horse
Remember my blue-black horse
Remember my blue-black horse
　　Remember my horse
　　Remember my horse
Remember
Remember

You know, they were company, & on their nights an
old man knew of something wonderful. A long time
ago he had seen a horse with horns. It was among
the wild horses at the place called Three Canada
He made a shield for her son, but her son was
killed, & the shield was lost

The Horned Horse Shield

Plainview: 3

The sun appearing: a pendant
of clear cutbeads, flashing;
a drift of pollen and glitter
lapping and overlapping night;
a prairie fire.

Plainview: 4

Johnnycake and venison and sassafras tea,
Johnnycake and venison and sassafras tea.

Just there another house, Poor Buffalo's house.
The paint is gone from the wood, and the people are
gone from the house. Once upon a time I saw the people
there, in the windows and the yard. An old woman
lived there, one of whose girlhood I have often dreamed.
She was Milly Durgan of Texas, and a Kiowa captive.

Aye, Milly Durgan, you've gone now to be
Away in the country and captivity;
Aye, Milly Durgan, you've gone from your home
Away to the prairie forever to roam.

The warm wind lies about the house in March,
and there is a music in it, as I have heard, an
American song.

And it's ladies to the center
and it's gents around the row,
and we'll rally round the canebrake
and shoot the buffalo.

The lines in italics are from two American folk songs, "The Texian
Boys," and "Shoot the Buffalo."

The Fear of Bo-talee

Bo-talee rode easily among his enemies, once, twice, three—and four times. And all who saw him were amazed, for he was utterly without fear; so it seemed. But afterwards he said: Certainly I was afraid. I was afraid of the fear in the eyes of my enemies.

The Horse That Died of Shame

Once there was a man who owned a fine hunting
horse. It was black and fast and afraid of nothing.
When it was turned upon an enemy it charged in a
straight line and struck at full speed; the man
need have no hand upon the rein. But, you know,
that man knew fear. Once during a charge he turned
that animal from its course. That was a bad thing.
The hunting horse died of shame.

—from *The Way to Rainy Mountain*

In the one color of the horse there were many colors.
And that evening it wheeled, riderless, and broke
away into the long distance, running at full speed.
And so it does again and again in my dreaming. It
seems to concentrate all color and light into the
final moment of its life, until it streaks the
vision plane and is indefinite, and shines vaguely
like the gathering of March light to a storm.

The Delight Song of Tsoai-talee

I am a feather on the bright sky
I am the blue horse that runs in the plain
I am the fish that rolls, shining, in the water
I am the shadow that follows a child
I am the evening light, the lustre of meadows
I am an eagle playing with the wind
I am a cluster of bright beads
I am the farthest star
I am the cold of the dawn
I am the roaring of the rain
I am the glitter on the crust of the snow
I am the long track of the moon in a lake
I am a flame of four colors
I am a deer standing away in the dusk
I am a field of sumac and the pomme blanche
I am an angle of geese in the winter sky
I am the hunger of a young wolf
I am the whole dream of these things

You see, I am alive, I am alive
I stand in good relation to the earth
I stand in good relation to the gods
I stand in good relation to all that is beautiful
I stand in good relation to the daughter of Tsen-tainte
You see, I am alive, I am alive

Sun Dance Shield

Mine is a dangerous shield;
there is anger in it,
there is boasting in it.

Mine is a beautiful shield;
there is yellow pollen in it,
there is red earth in it.

Mine is a sacred shield;
there is vision in it,
there is remembrance in it.

Mine is a powerful shield;
there is medicine in it,
there is a sun dance in it.

My life is in this shield,
my life is in this shield.

Headwaters

Noon in the intermountain plain:
There is scant telling of the marsh—
A log, hollow and weather-stained,
An insect at the mouth, and moss—
Yet waters rise against the roots,
Stand brimming to the stalks. What moves?
What moves on this archaic force
Was wild and welling at the source.

Rainy Mountain Cemetery

Most is your name the name of this dark stone.
Deranged in death, the mind to be inheres
Forever in the nominal unknown,
The wake of nothing audible he hears
Who listens here and now to hear your name.

The early sun, red as a hunter's moon,
Runs in the plain. The mountain burns and shines;
And silence is the long approach of noon
Upon the shadow that your name defines—
And death this cold, black density of stone.

Angle of Geese

How shall we adorn
Recognition with our speech?—
  Now the dead firstborn
Will lag in the wake of words.

Custom intervenes;
We are civil, something more:
  More than language means,
The mute presence mulls and marks.

Almost of a mind,
We take measure of the loss;
  I am slow to find
The mere margin of repose.

And one November
It was longer in the watch,
  As if forever,
Of the huge ancestral goose.

So much symmetry!—
Like the pale angle of time
  And eternity.
The great shape labored and fell.

Quit of hope and hurt,
It held a motionless gaze
  Wide of time, alert,
On the dark distant flurry.

The Gourd Dancer

Mammedaty, 1880–1932

1. THE OMEN

Another season centers on this place.
Like memory the blood congeals in it;
Like memory the sun recedes in time
Into the hazy, southern distances.

A vagrant heat hangs on the dark river,
And shadows turn like smoke. An owl ascends
Among the branches, clattering, remote
Within its motion, intricate with age.

2. THE DREAM

Mammedaty saw to the building of this house. Just
there, by the arbor, he made a camp in the old way.
And in the evening when the hammers had fallen silent
and there were frogs and crickets in the black grass—
and a low, hectic wind upon the pale, slanting plane
of the moon's light—he settled deep down in his
mind to dream. He dreamed of dreaming, and of the
summer breaking upon his spirit, as drums break upon
the intervals of the dance, and of the gleaming gourds.

3. THE DANCE

Dancing,
He dreams, he dreams—
The long wind glances, moves
Forever as a music to the mind;
The gourds are flashes of the sun.
He takes the inward, mincing steps
That conjure old processions and returns.

Dancing,
His moccasins,
His sash and bandolier
Contain him in insignia;
His fan is powerful, concise
According to his agile hand,
And holds upon the deep, ancestral air.

4. THE GIVEAWAY

Someone spoke his name, Mammedaty, in which
his essence was and is. It was a serious matter that his
name should be spoken there in the circle, among the
many people, and he was thoughtful, full of wonder,
and aware of himself and of his name. He walked
slowly to the summons, looking into the eyes of the man
who summoned him. For a moment they held each
other in close regard, and all about them there was
excitement and suspense.

Then a boy came suddenly into the circle, leading
a black horse. The boy ran, and the horse after him.
He brought the horse up short in front of Mammedaty,
and the horse wheeled and threw its head and cut
its eyes in the wild way. And it blew hard and quivered
in its hide so that light ran, rippling, upon its shoulders
and its flanks—and then it stood still and was calm.
Its mane and tail were fixed in braids and feathers, and
a bright red chief's blanket was draped in a roll over
its withers. The boy placed the reins in Mammedaty's
hands. And all of this was for Mammedaty, in his honor,
as even now it is in the telling, and will be, as long as
there are those who imagine him in his name.

New World

1.

First Man,
behold:
the earth
glitters
with leaves;
the sky
glistens
with rain.
Pollen
is borne
on winds
that low
and lean
upon
mountains.
Cedars
blacken
the slopes—
and pines.

2.

At dawn
eagles
hie and
hover
above
the plain
where light
gathers
in pools.
Grasses
shimmer
and shine.
Shadows
withdraw
and lie
away
like smoke.

3.

At noon
turtles
enter
slowly
into
the warm
dark loam.
Bees hold
the swarm.
Meadows
recede
through planes
of heat
and pure
distance.

4.

At dusk
the gray
foxes
stiffen
in cold;
blackbirds
are fixed
in the
branches.
Rivers
follow
the moon,
the long
white track
of the
full moon.

Carriers of the Dream Wheel

This is the Wheel of Dreams
Which is carried on their voices,
By means of which their voices turn
And center upon being.
It encircles the First World,
This powerful wheel.
They shape their songs upon the wheel
And spin the names of the earth and sky,
The aboriginal names.
They are old men, or men
Who are old in their voices,
And they carry the wheel among the camps,
Saying: Come, come,
Let us tell the old stories,
Let us sing the sacred songs.

The Stalker

Sampt'e drew the string back and back until he
felt the bow wobble in his hand, and he let the
arrow go. It shot across the long light of the
morning and struck the black face of a stone in the
meadow; it glanced then away towards the west,
limping along in the air; and then it settled down
in the grass and lay still. Sampt'e approached; he
looked at it with wonder and was wary; honestly he
believed that the arrow might take flight again;
so much of his life did he give into it.

The Colors of Night

1. WHITE

An old man's son was killed far away in the Staked
Plains. When the old man heard of it he went there
and gathered up the bones. Thereafter, wherever the
old man ventured, he led a dark hunting horse which
bore the bones of his son on its back. And the old
man said to whomever he saw: "You see how it is that
now my son consists in his bones, that his bones
are polished and so gleam like glass in the light
of the sun and moon, that he is very beautiful."

2. YELLOW

There was a boy who drowned in the river, near the
grove of thirty-two bois d'arc trees. The light
of the moon lay like a path on the water, and a glitter
of low brilliance shone in it. The boy looked at
it and was enchanted. He began to sing a song that
he had never heard before; only then, once, did he
hear it in his heart, and it was borne like a cloud
of down upon his voice. His voice entered into the
bright track of the moon, and he followed after it.
For a time he made his way along the path of the
moon, singing. He paddled with his arms and legs
and felt his body rocking down into the swirling
water. His vision ran along the path of light and
reached across the wide night and took hold of the
moon. And across the river, where the path led into
the shadows of the bank, a black dog emerged from
the river, shivering and shaking the water from its
hair. All night it stood in the waves of grass and
howled the full moon down.

3. BROWN

On the night before a flood, the terrapins move to
high ground. How is it that they know? Once there
was a boy who took up a terrapin in his hands and
looked at it for a long time, as hard as he could

look. He succeeded in memorizing the terrapin's face,
but he failed to see how it was that the terrapin
knew anything at all.

4. RED

There was a man who had got possession of a powerful
medicine. And by means of this medicine he made a
woman out of sumac leaves and lived with her for
a time. Her eyes flashed, and her skin shone like
pipestone. But the man abused her, and so his medicine
failed. The woman was caught up in a whirlwind and
blown apart. Then nothing was left of her but a
thousand withered leaves scattered in the plain.

5. GREEN

A young girl awoke one night and looked out into
the moonlit meadow. There appeared to be a tree;
but it was only an appearance; there was a shape
made of smoke; but it was only an appearance; there
was a tree.

6. BLUE

One night there appeared a child in the camp. No
one had ever seen it before. It was not bad-looking,
and it spoke a language that was pleasant to hear,
though none could understand it. The wonderful thing
was that the child was perfectly unafraid, as if
it were at home among its own people. The child got
on well enough, but the next morning it was gone,
as suddenly as it had appeared. Everyone was troubled.
But then it came to be understood that the child
never was, and everyone felt better. "After all,"
said an old man, "how can we believe in the child?
It gave us not one word of sense to hold on to. What
we saw, if indeed we saw anything at all, must have
been a dog from a neighboring camp, or a bear that
wandered down from the high country."

7. PURPLE

There was a man who killed a buffalo bull to no
purpose, only he wanted its blood on his hands. It
was a great, old, noble beast, and it was a long
time blowing its life away. On the edge of the night
the people gathered themselves up in their grief
and shame. Away in the west they could see the hump
and spine of the huge beast which lay dying along
the edge of the world. They could see its bright
blood run into the sky, where it dried, darkening,
and was at last flecked with flakes of light.

8. BLACK

There was a woman whose hair was long and heavy
and black and beautiful. She drew it about her
like a shawl and so divided herself from the world
that not even Age could find her. Now and then she
steals into the men's societies and fits her voice
into their holiest songs. And always, just there,
is a shadow which the firelight cannot cleave.

North Dakota, North Light

The cold comes about
among the sheer, lucent planes.

Rabbits rest in the foreground;
the sky is clenched upon them.

A glassy wind glances
from the ball of bone in my wrist
even as I brace myself,
and I cannot conceive
of summer;

and another man in me
stands for it,
wills even to remain,

figurative, fixed,

among the hard, hunchbacked rabbits,
among the sheer, shining planes.

Long Shadows at Dulce

1.

September is a long
Illusion of itself;
The elders bide their time.

2.

The sheep camps are lively
With children. The slim girls,
The limber girls, recline.

3.

November is the flesh
And blood of the black bear,
Dusk its bone and marrow.

4.

In the huddled horses
That know of perfect cold
There is calm, like sorrow.

Crows in a Winter Composition

This morning the snow,
The soft distances
Beyond the trees
In which nothing appeared—
Nothing appeared.
The several silences,
Imposed one upon another,
Were unintelligible.

I was therefore ill at ease
When the crows came down,
Whirling down and calling,
Into the yard below
And stood in a mindless manner
On the gray, luminous crust,
Altogether definite, composed,
In the bright enmity of my regard,
In the hard nature of crows.

Anywhere Is a Street
into the Night

Desire will come of waiting
Here at this window—I bring
An old urgency to bear
Upon me, and anywhere
Is a street into the night,
Deliverance and delight—
And evenly it will pass
Like this image on the glass.

The Burning

In the numb, numberless days
There were disasters in the distance,
Strange upheavals. No one understood them.
At night the sky was scored with light,
For the far planes of the planet buckled and burned.
In the dawns were intervals of darkness
On the scorched sky, clusters of clouds and eclipse,
And cinders descending.
Nearer in the noons
The air lay low and ominous and inert.
And eventually at evening, or morning, or midday,
At the sheer wall of the wood,
Were shapes in the shadows approaching,
Always, and always alien and alike.
And in the foreground the fields were fixed in fire,
And the flames flowered in our flesh.

The Wound

The wound gaped open;
it was remarkably like the wedge of an orange
when it is split, spurting.
He wanted to close the wound with a kiss,
to graft his mouth to the warm, wet tissue.
He kept about the wound, waiting
and deeply disturbed,
his fascination
like the inside of the wound itself,
deep, as deep almost as the life principle,
the irresistible force of being.
The force lay there in the rupture of the flesh,
there in the center of the wound.

Had he been God,
he should himself have inflicted the wound;
and he should have taken the wound gently,
gently in his hands, and placed it
among the most brilliant wildflowers
in the meadows of the mountains.

Forms of the Earth at Abiquiu

For Georgia O'Keeffe

I imagine the time of our meeting
There among the forms of the earth at Abiquiu,
And other times that followed from the one—
An easy conjugation of stories,
And late luncheons of wine and cheese.
All around there were beautiful objects,
Clean and precise in their beauty, like bone.
Indeed, bone: a snake in the filaments of bone,
The skulls of cows and sheep;
And the many smooth stones in the window,
In the flat winter light, were beautiful.
I wanted to feel the sun in the stones—
The ashen, far-flung winter sun.
And then, in those days, too,
I made you the gift of a small, brown stone,
And you described it with the tips of your fingers
And knew at once that it was beautiful—
At once, accordingly you knew,
As you knew the forms of the earth at Abiquiu:
That time involves them and they bear away,
Beautiful, various, remote,
In failing light, and the coming of cold.

The Gift

For Bobby Jack Nelson

Older, more generous,
We give each other hope.
The gift is ominous:
Enough praise, enough rope.

THE STRANGE AND TRUE STORY OF MY LIFE WITH BILLY THE KID

Two Figures

These figures moving in my rhyme,
Who are they? Death and Death's dog, Time.

A Word on Billy the Kid

Billy the Kid was born in New York City in 1859. He died at
Fort Sumner, New Mexico, in 1881, shot down in a dark room by
Patrick F. Garrett, Sheriff of Lincoln County. His real name was
Henry McCarty, though he assumed other names as it pleased him
to do so—Henry Antrim, Billy Antrim, William H. Bonney—but
he was known far and wide as "Billy the Kid," or simply, "The
Kid." He is said to have killed twenty-one men, one for each year
of his life. But it is difficult to ascertain the facts; few if any men
have lived more deeply in legend.

Sister Blandina Segale was born in Cicagna, Italy, in 1850. She
came to the United States as a young girl and entered the
motherhouse of the Sisters of Charity in Cincinnati. She was
missioned to the West in 1872. She kept a remarkable journal that
was published under the title *At the End of the Santa Fe Trail*, in
1948. In it she recounts two meetings with Billy the Kid, one at
Trinidad, Colorado, the other at Santa Fe. She died at Cincinnati
in 1941.

Billy the Kid's mother was married at least twice. Her second
marriage took place in Santa Fe, 1 March 1873. Her two sons, Joe
and Henry, were her witnesses.

All else of what follows is imagined; nonetheless, it is so.

1.
Riding Is an Exercise of the Mind

One autumn morning in 1946 I woke up at Jemez Pueblo. I had arrived there in the middle of the night and gone to sleep. I had no idea of the landscape, no sense of where in the world I was. Now, in the bright New Mexican morning, I began to look around and settle in. I had found the last, best home of my childhood.

When my parents and I moved to Jemez I was twelve years old. The world was a different place then, and Jemez was the most exotic corner within it. The village and the valley, the canyons and the mountains had been there from the beginning of time, waiting for me. So it seemed. Marco Polo in the court of Kublai Khan had nothing on me. I was embarked upon the greatest adventure of all; I had come to the place of my growing up.

The landscape was full of mystery and of life. The autumn was in full bloom. The sun cast a golden light upon the adobe walls and the cornfields; it set fire to the leaves of willows and cottonwoods along the river; and a fresh cold wind ran down from the canyons and carried the good scents of pine and cedar smoke, of bread baking in the beehive ovens, and of rain in the mountains. There were horses in the plain and angles of geese in the sky.

One November, on the feast of San Diego, Jemez took on all the colors of a Renaissance Fair. I lived on the southwest corner of the village, on the wagon road to San Ysidro. I looked southward into the plain; there a caravan of covered wagons reached as far as the eye could see. These were the Navajos, coming in from Torreon. I had never seen such a pageant; it was as if that whole, proud people, the *Diné*, had been concentrated into one endless migration. There was a great dignity to them, even in revelry. They sat tall in the wagons and on horseback, going easily with laughter and singing their riding songs. And when they set up camp in the streets, they were perfectly at home, their dogs about them. They made coffee and fried bread and roasted mutton on their open fires.

Gradually and without effort I entered into the motion of life there. In the winter dusk I heard coyotes barking away by the river, the sound of the drums in the kiva, and the voice of the village crier, ringing at the rooftops.

And on summer nights of the full moon I saw old men in their ceremonial garb, running after witches—and sometimes I saw the witches themselves in the forms of bats and cats and owls on fence posts.

I came to know the land by going out upon it in all seasons, getting into it until it became the very element in which I lived my daily life.

I had a horse named Pecos, a fleet-footed roan gelding, which was my great glory for a time. Pecos could outrun all the other horses in the village, and he wanted always to prove it. We two came to a good understanding of each other, I believe. I did a lot of riding in those days, and I got to be very good at it. My Kiowa ancestors, who were centaurs, should have been proud of me.

Riding is an exercise of the mind. I dreamed a good deal on the back of my horse, going out into the hills alone. Desperados were everywhere in the brush. More than once I came upon roving bands of hostile Indians and had, on the spur of the moment, to put down an uprising. Now and then I found a wagon train in trouble, and always among the settlers there was a lovely young girl from Charleston or Philadelphia who needed simply and more than anything else in the world to be saved. I saved her.

After a time Billy the Kid was with me on most of those adventures. He rode on my right side and a couple of steps behind. I watched him out of the corner of my eye, for he bore watching. We got on well together in the main, and he was a good man to have along in a fight. We had to be careful of glory-seeking punks. Incredibly there were those in the world who were foolish enough to oppose us, merely for the sake of gaining a certain reputation.

When it came time for me to leave home and venture out into the wider world, I sold my horse to an old gentleman at Vallecitos. I like to think that Pecos went on with our games long afterwards, that in his old age he listened for the sound of bugles and of gunfire—and for the pitiful weeping of young ladies in distress—and that he heard them as surely as I do now.

2.
Billy the Kid,
His Rocking Horse:
A Lullaby

Ride, Billy, Billy,
Ride, Billy, ride;
Ride about the countryside.

Sing, Billy, Billy,
Sing, Billy, sing;
Sing a song of galloping.

Whoa, Billy, Billy,
Whoa, Billy, whoa;
Hold your horse and let him blow.

Sleep, Billy, Billy,
Sleep, Billy, sleep;
May your sleep be dark and deep.

3.

Billy the Boy at Silver City

Already, in the sultry streets,
the mean quotient of suspicion
settles at his crooked mouth, but
just inside himself, he perceives,
in the still landscape of legend,
the cold of his dark destiny;
already, in the sultry streets,
he resembles himself in death.

4.

Henry McCarty Witnesses His Mother's Marriage, 1 March 1873

She is pale, lovely, and lithe.
Her sons are stiff and homely,
And they make hard witnesses.
Joe is careless, distant, dumb;
Henry imagines marriage,
The remorse and agonies
Of age. He looks upon her,
His mother, and his mind turns
Upon him; the beautiful
His example of despair.

5.
The Man in Black

I rode across the snowfields in the moonlight, holding myself in steady relation to the stars. The black timber on either side lay flat against the slopes, running down before me into the bottom of the night. In the dusk I had seen rabbits—and once a fox, like the point of a flame, flickering among the trees. But now for miles I had seen nothing but the night. There were wolves about; I believed in them, for the near edge of their presence cut into the nerves of my horse, and our going on was quiet and cautious. And it was cold; the cold was absolute. At length nothing mattered, not even the wolves, because of the cold. At nine o'clock, perhaps, I saw the lights at Arroyo Seco.

The man sitting across the table from me was slight of build and rather unseemly in appearance. He affected the wearing of black, which in another, more imposing figure might have been dramatic, even ominous; but in this man it was an unremarkable aspect, save that it accentuated something that lay deeper than his appearance, a certain somberness, a touch of grief. It was as if the Angel of Death had long ago found out his name. His skin was nearly colorless, and his front teeth protruded to such an extent that his thin lips seemed never to come together. His eyes were blue, just the blue of water in milk, and devoid of expression, so that it was impossible to say what he was thinking—or indeed *that* he was thinking. Thought seemed somehow irrelevant to his real being, apart from his true nature. I have heard that certain organisms—sharks, for example—are virtually mindless, that they are creatures of pure instinct. So it was with this man, I believe. If a rational thought, or a whole emotion, had ever grown up inside of him, he should have suffered a great dislocation of himself in his mind and soul. Such was my impression; he should have been like a plate of glass that is shattered upon a stone. But at the same time I had the sense that his instincts were nearly infallible. Nothing should ever take him by surprise—and no one, except perhaps himself. Only one principle motivated him, that of survival—his own mean and exclusive survival. For him there was no morality in the universe but that, neither choice nor question. And for that reason he was among the deadliest creatures on the face of the earth.

His hands were remarkably small and delicately formed. I have heard it said that they were like a woman's hands, and with respect to size and shape that is true. But they were rough, too, and marked by hard use. There was something like propriety in all their attitudes—and great utility; you looked at them and you thought at once of fine tools, precision instruments. They were steady and extraordinarily expressive. You could read this man in his hands as you could never read him in his eyes. His hands articulated him in the way that a leaf articulates the wind or the current of a stream. And yet they were nearly evasive, too, in their propriety.

There was no resonance in his voice, but it was thin and hard and flat—wood clacking lightly upon wood. He was ill at ease within the element of language; I believe that silence was his natural habitat. Notwithstanding, his speech was plain and direct—and disarmingly polite.

"Thank you for coming," he said.

"I will go with you," I replied.

And this is how it began; and this is the strange and true story of my life with Billy the Kid.

6.
He Reckons Geologic Time According to His Sign

He finds a fossil fish
There in the riverbed.
He wonders about it;
It is a long time dead.

The fish descends in rock,
As if the sheer incline
Might slant its destiny
According to some sign.

So Sagittarius
Must swim against the tide.
He reckons upon time,
And time is on his side.

His legend is secure;
He bodies resistance.
The fossil is himself,
His own indifference.

7.

A Prospector Catches Sight of Him in the Doña Anas

He wanders in the high desert
Like a coyote. The wind burns him.
His spirit is a brittle limb,
His instincts languor and alert.

8.
On the Simple Nature of His Lust

Among the wily whoremongers,
Wily Billy thirsts and hungers
For woman: she determines him.
In scent and paint and feather trim
She holds him in her subtle sway.
He is determined anyway.

9.

The Girl at the Doll House

They say the whores
are indolent
at the Doll House
where he has been

A sometime guest.
He remembers
a girl whose hands
distracted him.

Her hands were long,
soft and supple;
nor were they drawn
with dread. She said,

"Will you come back?"
And he answered,
"No." Nonetheless
he remembers:

Indolence lay
cold and benign
in her white hands
and hardened there.

10.
Billy's Boast to an Old Blind Woman at San Patricio

I am the desperado of these parts;
I deal in felonies and broken hearts.

11.
He Counts Anacita the Weaver Among His True Loves

In Mesilla he sees a woman weave;
He loves her, and his heart is on his sleeve.

But she is lost to him. Her husband stands
Between them, holding vengeance in his hands.

12.
Billy the Kid Offers a Kindness
to an Old Man at Glorieta

He was a broken-down old man, a twist of rawhide. When you looked at him you had the sense that you were looking at a ruin, something of prehistoric character, like a shard of pottery or the remnant of an ancient wall. His face, especially, was an archaeology in itself. The shadows of epochs come and go in such a face.

He was a cowboy, he allowed. He had broken horses all his life, and not a few of them had broken him. And he had known men and women, good and bad—singular men and singular women. He was more than willing to talk about these and other things. We listened, Billy and I. The old man's real existence was at last invested in his stories; there he lived, and not elsewhere. He was nothing so much as the story of himself, the telling of a tale to which flesh was gathered incidentally. It was no wonder Billy liked him.

We passed the time of day with him, and he created us over and over again in his stories, fashioned us into myriad wonderful things that we should not otherwise have been. Now we were trick-shot artists in a Wild West Show, and the old man, his guns blazing, shot the buttons off our vests. Again we dined on the most exotic and delicious fruits in the golden palaces of the Orient. We were there at the Battle of the Wilderness, at the very point of the Bloody Angle, following the old man into legend. Christmas was coming on, and we were the Magi, the old man said. Laughing, we half believed him. And then it was time to go.

Billy fetched a plug of tobacco from his coat pocket, cut it in two with a jackknife, and gave the old man half. We said goodbye and left the old man there at Glorieta, before his fire. The leading edge of a dream was moving like a distant, migrant bird across his eyes.

Later, on the way to Santa Fe, I said to Billy:

"Say, amigo, I have never seen you chew tobacco."

"No, and it isn't likely that you ever will," he said. "I have no use for the weed."

Then, seeing that I was perplexed, he went on:

"I bought the tobacco at La Junta because I knew that we were coming this way and I hoped to see the old man, who is my true friend. He has a taste for it. And I offered him the half instead of the whole because he should prefer that I did not give him something outright; it pleased him that I should share something of my own with him. As it happens, I have thrown away my share, in which the ownership consists—it lies back there in a snowdrift. But that is an unimportant matter, a trivial conceit— and this the old man understands and appreciates more even than the tobacco itself."

He started to say something more, but apparently he thought better of it and fell silent. He seemed lost in thought, but it was impossible to say. This brief sojourn into language had been for him extraordinary, and he seemed spent, and indeed almost remorseful and contrite, as if he had squandered something of which he had too little in store. His eyes were precisely equal in color to the sky at that moment, and the sky was curdled with snow.

"Indeed we are the Magi," I said, but I said it softly, that his thoughts, whatever they were, should not be disturbed.

13.

He Encounters a Player at Words

Come down, Billy, to Lincoln town;
Come down, you Kid of great renown.
All right, Patrick, I'll come with you.
And then, pray tell, what will we do?
We'll dance a jig and dine on shoat,
And you shall be my billy goat.

14.

He Would Place a Chair for Sister Blandina

They had met at Trinidad,
The nun and the renegade;
They had measured each other
And exchanged confidences.
He was simply chivalrous,
She thought; she prudent, he thought.
Precisely, they got on well.

And now, in her charity,
After years, she comes to him
At the jail in Santa Fe.
There is nothing in his eyes;
He is shackled, hand and foot.
Still, he regards her. "I wish
I could place a chair for you,
Sister." And she regards him.
Later she will weep for him.

15.
Billy Fixes a Bully in His Gaze

One day Billy and I were riding down from the high country
south of the Hondo Valley. It was getting on towards evening,
and the light was failing fast. Far below we could see the pale
geometry of a village, Arroyo Corvo, as I recall, and we made
straight for the cantina there. Night came on as we stood,
without talking, at the bar. An hour passed, and another; then:
   "Move over, friend."
   A thick, bearded man stepped between us, facing Billy.
Quite apart from the fact that he was obviously drunk, there was
something repulsive in his manner. You could see at once that
there was no steel in him—and not a glimmer of the doom that was
about to fall on him. I caught my breath. Over the intruder's
shoulder I saw Billy raise his eyes, slowly. He said nothing,
nor did he give so much as an inch, but for a moment his eyes lay
upon the man like a shroud, and he returned to his drink. The
man withered away. I had never seen Billy fix a man in his gaze
before. For years now I have tried to understand what it was
that I saw in his eyes at that moment. There are times when
it seems surely to have been something like sorrow, a faintest
sadness. But at other times I realize that there was nothing,
nothing at all, that Billy was the only man I have ever known
in whose eyes there was no expression whatsoever.

16.
Trees and Evening Sky

He saw the black trees leaning
In different ways, their limbs
Tangled on the mottled clouds,
The clouds rolling on themselves;
A wide belt of four colors,
Yellow, orange, red, and black;
And stars in the tangled limbs.

17.

He Foretells Disaster in a Dream

I wanted just to speak,
To mutter or cry out;
I wanted just to see
My vagrant enemy—

Vagrant as the pale streak
Of evening, come about
On the plane of winter,
The long, crystal splinter

Of despair. Now the bleak
Dimension of my doubt
Comprehends me. I wake
And waken for my sake.

18.

He Enters Upon the Afternoon of His Last Day

But then and there the sun bore down
And was a focal length away.
The brain was withered and burned brown,
Then gone to ashes, cold and gray.

19.

Billy the Kid, the Departure of His Soul, 14 July 1881

There where I watch you walk
In quiet and in dark,
To where your time has come
   And you grow old
In ignorance and vain;

There where I hear the shot,
In quiet and in dark,
I think of what you think
   And of the cold
That fixes you in thought;

There where you are not, yet,
In quiet and in dark
I imagine you there
   And you appear
And are indefinite.

20.
Wide Empty Landscape with a Death in the Foreground

Here are weeds about his mouth;
His teeth are ashes.

It is this which succeeds him:
This huge, barren plain.

For him there is no question
Of elsewhere. His place

Is just this reality,
This deep element.

Now that he is dead he bears
Upon the vision

Merely, without resistance.
Death displaces him

No more than life displaced him;
He was always here.

21.
Two Figures

These figures moving in my rhyme,
Who are they? Death and Death's dog, Time.

✸ IN THE PRESENCE OF THE SUN

A GATHERING OF SHIELDS

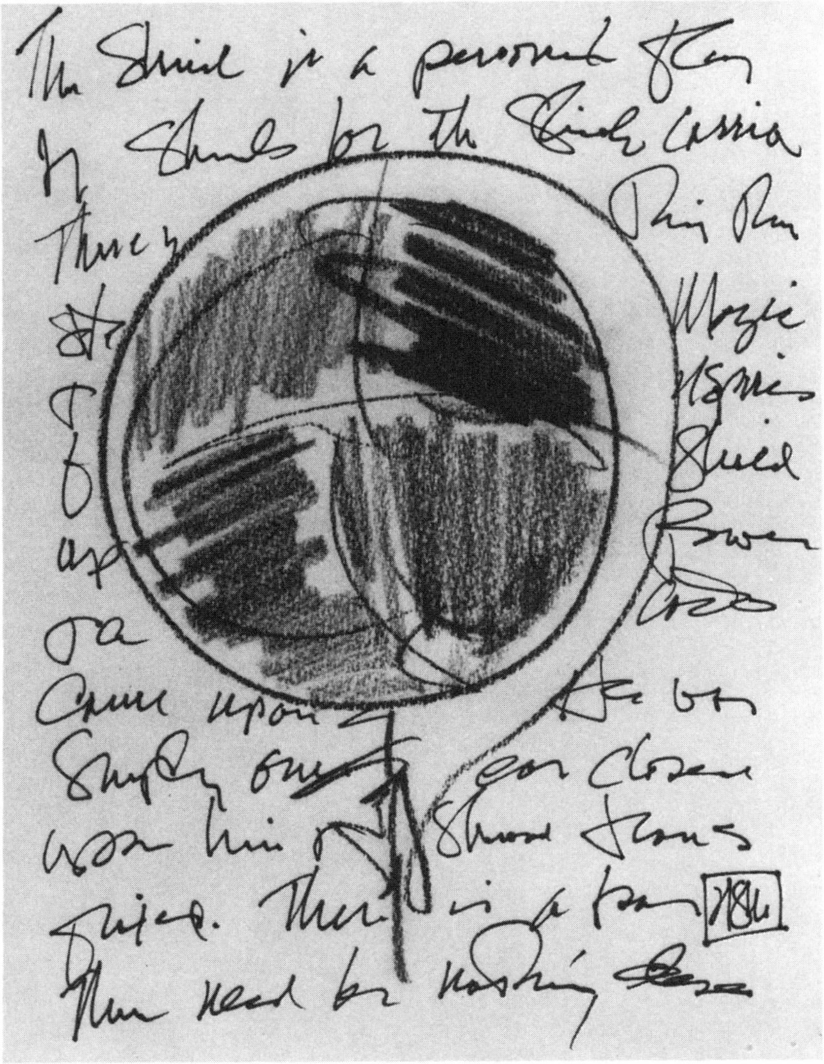

The Story of a Well-Made Shield

Now in the dawn before it dies, the eagle swings
low and wide in a great arc, curving downward
to the place of origin. There is no wind, but
there is a long roaring on the air. It is like the
wind—nor is it quite like the wind—but more
powerful.

A Word on the Plains Shield

Oyate awicahipi kin hehan lyou waslahy el wasicu wan Ble
eciyape ci Jack Carrigan kici mazopiye yuhapi ca he Sitting Bull's
shield kiu he opeton. Mr. One Bull says he can draw the shield.
Please send him paper and colors. Green grass color, dark blue,
brown scarlet. Yes Sitting Bull's father Jumping Bull gave him
this shield and named him Sitting Bull. Jumping Bull made this
shield from a vision. When Sitting Bull wears his shield he paints
his horse in a certain way. Yes his father gave him this painting.
When they have a shield they are not supposed to tell a lie or
think wrong. If they do they are wounded or killed. When
Sitting Bull's band was brought to the Standing Rock Agency, a
white man, in a store with Jack Carrigan, by the name of Billie
(William McNider) bought Sitting Bull's shield.

> *"With Regard to Sitting Bull,"*
> *Given by His Nephew, One Bull,*
> *and Transcribed by His Grandniece,*
> *Mrs. Cecelia One Bull Brown*

In its basic form the Plains shield is round and made of durable
materials. It is relatively small and light in weight. A diameter
of twenty-four inches is close to the average. The manufacture
consists of hide and adornments. The hide is thick and dried to a
remarkable hardness; it is most often the hide of a bison. Only
in a limited sense can the shield rightly be considered armor,
although it is strong enough to repel missiles, stones and clubs
certainly, but also arrows and even balls and bullets shot from

firearms, especially if the blow is glancing. But first and above all the shield is medicine.

The Plains shield reflects the character of the Plains culture, also known as the Horse culture or Centaur culture. It evidences a nomadic society and a warrior ideal. Those who carried shields were hunters and fighters whose purpose it was to raid, to capture, and to demonstrate extraordinary bravery.

The aesthetic aspect of the Plains shield is pronounced; the shield is a unique work of art. Without exception great care is given to the decoration of a proper shield. The artwork on many Plains shields is highly evolved in terms of proportion, design, symmetry, color, and imagination. Plains shield art is the equal of the great ledgerbook drawings of the nineteenth century, which in turn have been compared to Archaic Greek vase painting. It is an art of high order and singular accomplishment.

The shield bears a remarkable relationship to the individual to whom it belongs. Indeed the relationship is so immediate, so intimate as to be virtually impossible to define. In a real sense the Plains warrior *is* his shield. It is his personal flag, the realization of his vision and his name, the object of his holiest quest, the tangible expression of his deepest being. In bearing his shield he says, "My shield stands for me, and I stand for my shield. I am, and I am my shield!"

The shield is a mask. The mask is an appearance that discloses reality beyond appearance. Like other masks, it bespeaks sacred mystery. The shield is what you see, believes the Plains warrior. It reflects your own reality, as it does mine, he says. It reveals to you the essence of your self. It charms you, frightens you, disarms you, renders you helpless. You behold my shield, and you are transfixed or transformed, perhaps inspired beyond your imagining. Nothing will ever be the same again, for you have entered into the presence of my power. Oh, my enemy! Behold my shield!

The shield is involved in story. The shield is its own story. When the shield is made visible it means: Here is the story. Enter into it and be created. The story tells of your real being.

The shields in this gathering exist quintessentially in the element of language, and they are directly related to the stories, songs, spells, charms, and prayers of the Native American oral tradition. Here are sixteen shields, a quantity that is deeply meaningful, for it is predicated upon the sacred number four. The shields make four fours.

And the shields are meditations that make a round of life. The shield stories are meant to be told aloud, either to oneself or to another or to others, one each day for sixteen consecutive days, in which on the fourth, eighth, twelfth, and sixteenth days the storyteller and his listener or listeners might fast in order to be hale and worthy and pure in spirit. The stories ought to be told in the early morning or late afternoon, when the sun is close to the horizon, and always in the presence of the sun.

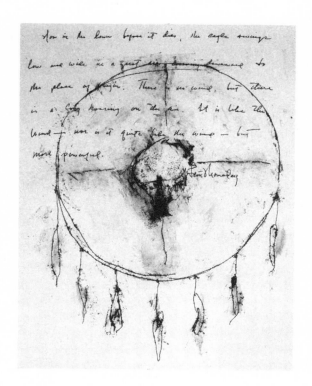

The Shattered Sky Shield

In the winter of 1833 the stars fell. The people were terribly frightened, and they ran about screaming and tearing at their hair. Only one man, old man Give Him Back, was unafraid. When the commotion began, he came out of his tepee and sat down on the ground on his crossed legs and observed the brilliant havoc overhead. The cold, black winter sky was everywhere shot through with fiery, streaming light. It seemed that the whole roof of the world was falling down. The panic mounted, but old man Give Him Back held on to himself and was watchful. He was not altogether calm, mind you, but he was attentive, *appreciative*. Afterwards, looking upon the shield he had made, he said to his wife Blue Hoof, "I wanted to see it all, the shattering of the sky, to take it all inside of me. My old eyes were hungry for it. I was so curious, so taken with wonder and fearful delight—for the first time since I was a child. I was like a puppy snapping at the butterflies."

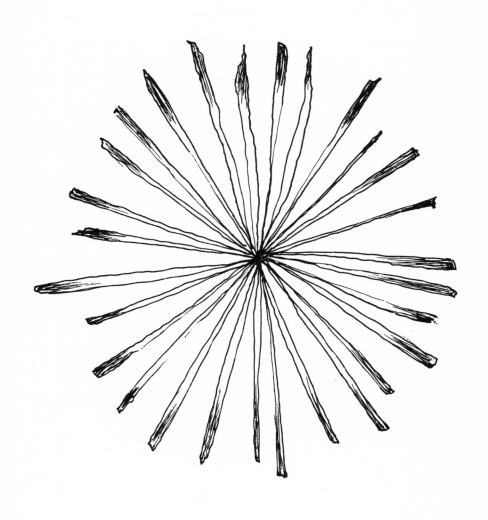

The Shield That Came Back

Turning Around tested his son Yellow Grass. "You must kill thirty scissortails and make me a fan of their feathers."

"Must I make the whole fan?" asked Yellow Grass. "Must I do the beadwork too?" Yellow Grass had never made a fan.

"Yes. You must do the beadwork too—blue and black and white and orange."

"Those are the colors of your shield," said Yellow Grass.

Yellow Grass fretted over the making of his father's fan, but when at last it was finished it was a fine, beautiful thing, the feathers tightly bunched and closely matched, their sheen like a rainbow—yet they could be spread wide in a disc, like a shield. And the handle was beaded tightly. The blue and black and white and orange beads glittered in every light. And there was a long bunch of doeskin fringes at the handle's end.

When Turning Around saw the fan he said nothing, but he was full of pride and admiration. Then he went off on a raiding expedition to the Pueblo country, and there he was killed. After that, Yellow Grass went among the Pueblos and redeemed his father's shield. But the fan could not be found.

When he was an old man Yellow Grass said to his grandson Handsome Horse, "You see, the shield was more powerful than the fan, for the shield came back and the fan did not. Some things, if they are very powerful, come back. Remember that. For us, in this camp, that is how to think of the world."

The Floating Feathers Shield

When Gai-talee was still a boy, learning how to hunt, he had a wonderful dream. In it he saw a great bear on the side of a mountain. The bear stood still for a long time, waiting in the shadow of a high stone ridge near timberline. Then a shape hurtled on the ridge, and the bear reared suddenly and took in his claws an eagle from the air. For a moment there was an awful frenzy; then again the stillness, and dark feathers floating and fluttering down on a little wind.

Gai-talee told Many Magpies of the shield he wanted, and it was made according to his dream. Gai-talee raided many times in Mexico, and he carried his shield with him. They say that Gai-talee's shield is well known below the Llano Estacado.

Bote-talee's Shield

Bote-talee found the Spider Woman. In the early morning he went swimming. When he reached the bank he looked directly up into the sun. There, just before his eyes, was a spider's web. It was a luminous, glistening shield. Bote-talee looked at it for a long time. It was so beautiful that he wanted to cry. He wondered if it were strong as well as beautiful. He flung water upon it, heavy water, again and again, but it remained whole and glistened all the more.

Then a sun spider entered upon the web. "Spider Woman," Bote-talee said, "Will you give me this perfect shield?"

"Bote-talee," said Spider Woman, "This is your shield."

The Sun Dance Shield

Long ago, when dogs could talk, Burning Boy brought home a woman from the Crow country. She was handsome and strong, and her name was Roan Calf. Burning Boy told his father that in a dream a dog had described the woman to him and told him where she could be found; she would make him a proper wife.

Among Roan Calf's possessions was a shield that had belonged to her late husband, who had died at Blue Meadows. It was a Sun Dance shield, and Burning Boy's father placed it in a ceremonial tepee along with the most powerful medicines in the tribe.

The woman Roan Calf lived a long time and was greatly loved and respected in Burning Boy's camp. The shield was exposed during the annual Sun Dance.

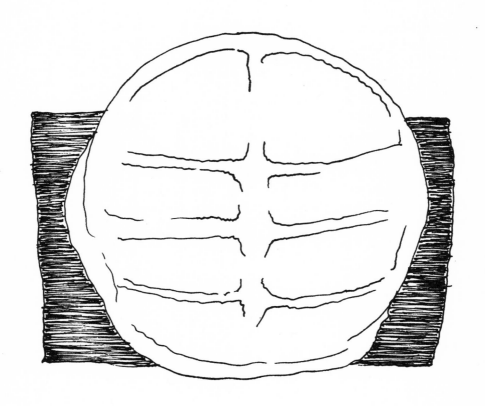

The Plainest of Shields

Akeah-de. They were camping near Bent's Fort. There was
a man whose right arm and hand were useless. He was called
Crow Neck, and he had been wounded in a battle with the
Utes. He had very nearly lost his life. Both before and
after the fight there were those who chided him for not
painting his shield. "It is not a strong shield," they said.
"It did not save you from being hurt, after all. Had you
painted your shield in the proper way, you would no doubt
still have the use of your arm and hand." But Crow Neck
only shrugged and replied, "From my point of view my shield
saved my life. From now on I shall carry it so." Formerly
he had carried the shield on his left arm. Now he suspended
it by means of a strap over his right shoulder; it covered
his crippled limb. His enemies were distracted by his shield,
carried so, and yet it was not a distracting thing in itself.
It was the plainest of shields.

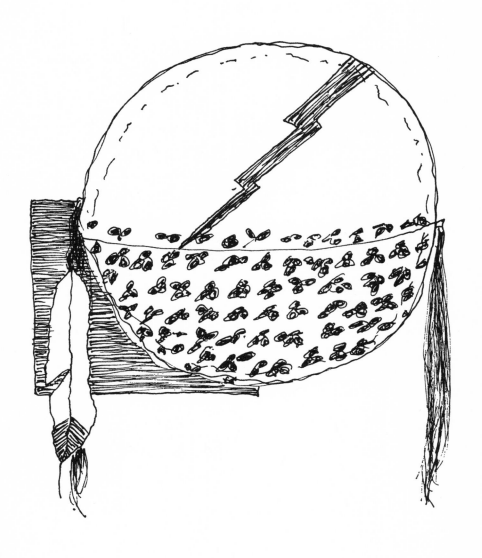

The Shield of the Time
of the Bluebonnets

That year they stole a child whose name was Christian far
to the south and east, where there were great fields of
bluebonnets, more than the war party had ever seen. The
man who brought Christian back was Mas o Menos, himself
a captive. Mas o Menos raised Christian as his son and made
for him a shield out of horsehide, with long strands of
horsehair fixed to it. It was a likely shield, bearing the
bright image of a bolt of lightning striking down in a meadow
of bluebonnets, and everyone admired it. Christian kept
it all his life, but he did not live so long as his adoptive
father. It was buried with Mas o Menos in 1922. When Mas
o Menos died, they say, he held tightly to the shield and
promised to carry it safely to his beloved son Christian.

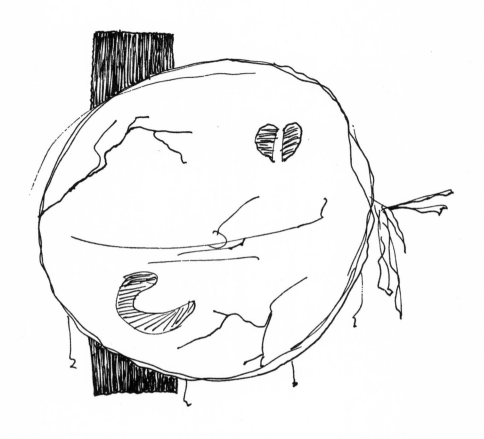

The Shield of Which the Less Said the Better

A man—his name is of no importance—owned a shield. The shield came down in the man's family. The man's grandson carried the shield into a fight at Stinking Creek, and he was killed. Soldiers took away the shield. Some years ago old man Red Horn bought the shield in a white man's store at Clinton, Oklahoma, for seventeen dollars. The shield was worth seventeen dollars, more or less.

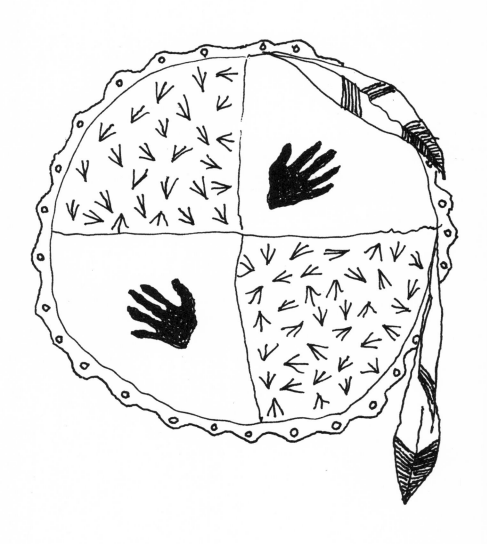

The Shield That Died

There was a man whose shield was made of willow and horsehide
and feathers and paint. The decoration was wonderful—the
footprints of a lizard on a yellow field, the hands of an
enemy on a blue field. One day the man carried the shield
off to the west. He was going hunting, he said. But when
he returned, he appeared in the camp without his shield.
No one wanted to ask him directly what had happened to the
shield, but everyone imagined that he had lost it because
he was a coward; in the face of death he had thrown it away
and fled. He lived to be very old, and no one ever knew
the true story of the shield. The people regarded the man
with sorrow and misgiving, and they said to visitors that
his shield had died.

Walking Bear's Shield

There were many berries that summer. The people camped in the Black Hills. Oh, you should have seen the camps! They were even better, brighter than sunlit stones in a mountain stream.

In those days bears were all about. A bear came walking among the camps. The men, you know, would have killed the bear under different circumstances. But the bear was unafraid. Certainly the bear was not hungry, for berries were abundant in the hills, but it came, anyway, into the camps, and it did not threaten the people. It walked through the circles of tepees, and it paused before the tepee of Otters Going On. Everyone watched; everyone was amazed.

When the wife of Otters Going On gave birth to a male child, Otters Going On made a shield for him, a very powerful bear shield. Setmaunt, Walking Bear, the son of Otters Going On, carried the shield far and wide.

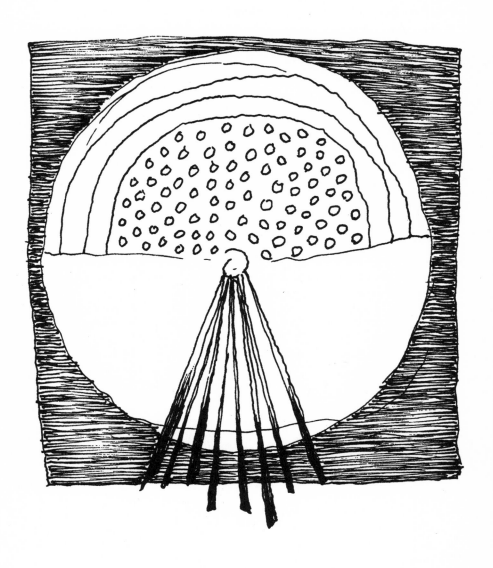

The Shield of Pai-matone's Brother

A young boy was captured in Texas and raised in the Little Kettle family. His name was Elijah, but the people did not like that name, for it was hard for them to say. He was called therefore Pai-matone's Brother. Pai-matone of the Little Kettles was a very beautiful young woman.

When Pai-matone's Brother had grown into a young man, he saw a strange thing: a rainbow reaching out almost horizontally on the north sky above the Smoky Hill River. And one band of the rainbow's colors was violet, the very color of the canyons east of the Staked Plains. He told Pai-matone of what he had seen. "My sister," he said, "I want to set that color upon my shield."

Pai-matone searched far and wide for the color, and at last she found it in the clay banks of the Smoky Hill River. The rainbow lay buried there.

The Shield That Was Touched
by Pretty Mouth

Waterstrider was the son of Crooked Back, and like his father he
was crippled from birth. He could not stand straight up but must
be always bent like a juniper twig. In the time of the spilling moon
he kept to himself on the river, grieving over the death of the girl
Pretty Mouth, who had been trampled by horses. Enemies came to
the river, and Waterstrider frightened them away with his shield,
stealing two of their best weapons. His shield was made by Many
Magpies, a young man among the shieldmakers.

   In the night, in the moonlit water, the girl Pretty Mouth
appeared to Waterstrider. She was beautiful and graceful beyond
his belief. Her supple body was curved and shone like the moon.
She approached upon the bank and stood very close to
Waterstrider. She reached out and touched her fingers to the
shield. And then the time of Waterstrider's grief was ended.

The Shield That Was Looked After by Dogs

The shield belonged to Long Feet. The whole story of the
shield is unknown; this is what is known. Long Feet was
a dreamer. He lived alone, away from the camps. He was a
hermit, and he kept among the dogs. He was thought to be
very wise, and he was admired for his independence. He never
married, nor did he have children. His shield, which was
old and powerful, was found near Rainy Mountain, where Long
Feet died of old age. Four dogs were looking after it. They
had to be spoken to in a sorrowful, respectful way.

The Muddy Horses Shield

There was a succession of great storms, and the plains were sodden. The horses had a hard time moving about. Buffalo Beard was a young man at the time. As a boy he had dreamed of taking part in a glorious raid, and so it happened. The horses were mired in mud, and the warriors were afraid. But Buffalo Beard led the raid on foot, and it was successful. According to a calendar that was kept by his wife Sees-the-Sun, Buffalo Beard counted two coups. This was in the land of the snake hunters. Many Magpies made the shield. It bears the stark image of a standing horse without feet. It is decorated with horse hair and chips from a horse's hoof.

The Shield That Was Brought Down from Tsoai

It came to this: that Many Dogs so loved a horse that belonged to Dragonfly that he could not sleep. He wanted more than anything in the world to have that horse for himself. One day he said to Dragonfly, "Please, will you give me that horse in trade?"

"Well, no . . . well, I don't know," said Dragonfly. "What will you give me for the horse?"

"I will give you my grandfather's shield," said Many Dogs, "the ancient shield that was brought down from Tsoai."

"Haw!" Dragonfly was amazed, and all of his shrewdness was put aside. "That is a famous shield," he said.

"Yes," said Many Dogs.

"The horse is a hunter," said Dragonfly in spite of himself. "It is a big, fast, black-eared hunter." He need not have said it, and he was ashamed.

"Yes, I know," replied Many Dogs. "Will you trade?"

"All right," said Dragonfly.

The end of the story is that Dragonfly gave Many Dogs eight horses for the shield that was brought down from Tsoai.

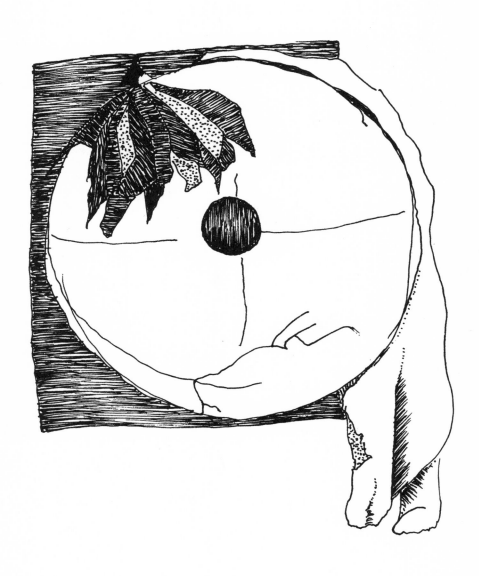

The Shield of Two Dreams

Dark Water started from her sleep, listening hard, holding her breath. There was, at a distance, the sound of a running horse, of hooves chipping rapidly at the hard winter ground. Strangely, there was no urgency in it, only the flat rapping of the hooves, the right rhythm of a running horse. It grew louder, then fainter; and then it was no more. She had not even thought of crying out. Then it occurred to her that no one else had heard. Her mother and father, her two sisters were there, almost within her reach, and they had not heard. They breathed easily in their sleep. Not one dog in the whole camp had heard. There was now only a deep, silent wake.

The next morning Dark Water told her father Green Shirt of what she had heard. "It approached as close as the stand of willows on Hungry Child Creek," she said. Green Shirt said nothing at first, setting his face in a frown. Then he said, "I dreamed of this before you were born, of a shield with owl feathers." And, sure enough, in the stand of willows there was the shield. It was very old and beautiful. "The shield was revealed to me in a dream long ago," said Green Shirt, "but it came to me at last in your dream. Now, when I hold it up to others, to my friends and enemies, I shall say, 'This is my shield, and this is my daughter's shield! Behold!'"

Planned Parenthood

If coupling should but make us whole
And of the selfsame mind and soul,
Then couple let's in celebration;
We have contained the population.

The Death of Beauty

She died a beauty of repute,
Her other virtues in dispute.

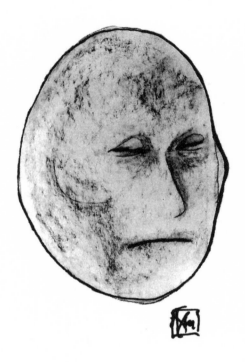

On Futility

He worked hard and was rewarded.
His reward is here recorded.

On Chastity

Here lies a lady sweet and chaste.
Here lies the matter: chaste makes waste.

Of Ambition

He drove himself, and was undone,
And left no stone unturned but one.

On the Cause of a Homely Death

Even the echoes are instilled
In dust. Imagine it was age
And worthy destiny fulfilled,
Not fear, not loneliness, not rage.

The Great Fillmore Street
Buffalo Drive

Insinuate the sun through fog
upon Pacific Heights, upon the man on horseback,
upon the herd ascending. *There* is color and clamor.

And there he waves them down,
those great, humpbacked animals,
until their wild grace gone
they lumber and lunge
and blood blisters at their teeth,
and their hooves score the street—

and among boulders they settle on the sea.

He looks after them, twisted round upon his sorrow,
the drape of his flag now full and formal,
ceremonial.

One bull, animal representation of the sun,
he dreams back from the brink
to the green refuge of his hunter's heart.
It grazes near a canyon wall,
along a ribbon of light, among redbud trees,
eventually into shadow.

Then the hold of his eyes is broken:
on the farther rim the grasses flicker and blur,
a hawk brushes rain across the dusk,
meadows recede into mountains, and here and there
are moons like salmonberries
upon the glacial face of the sky.

Girl with umbrella

Marina Green

For Reina, Valentine's Day, 1981

The kites darted in the wind at early evening.
They were of different, dark colors.

A woman in a long coat brought her hand up,
the fingers to a corner of her mouth,

and shadows ran upon and overcame the waves.
A seagull held almost still beyond the kites.

That was another time. The scene was livelier—
or was it not? And you, are you that same woman?

Nous avons vu la mer

We have been lovers,
you and I.
We have been alive
in the clear mornings of Genesis;
in the afternoons,
among the prisms of the air,
our hands have shaped perfect silences.
We have seen the sea;
wonder is well known to us.

A Fire at Thule

For weeks now the sun has risen and set;
There has been an ordinary commerce.

The city sounds. Old people come and go,
The streets are colored with cartons and cans.

My little daughter speaks of you. She says
You are sad, you have done with make-believe.

The having done is hard to my ear, my
Having done with the urgency to lie.

Make believe. Imagine the sky becomes
The sea, a fire at Thule, your having been.

Play at the time that was, the dawn to be,
The dusk in which is faded our concern,

The frozen field between us, the incline
Upon which loss is suffered, and we grieve.

Wreckage

Had my bones, like the sun,
been splintered on this canyon wall
and burned among these buckled plates,
this bright debris; had it been so,
I should not have lingered so long
among my losses. I should have come
loudly, like a warrior, to my time.

Old Guerre

For Janet

BERTRANDE: *Is he not aged?*
CATHERINE: *Yes, Mistress. Greatly aged.*
BERTRANDE: *Resentment burdens the heart.*
CATHERINE: *And the body keeps time with the heart.*

Against his will old Guerre thinks of his son:
You gall me, and I am grown old. You never were.
But, yes, you were. Maybe you are, among soldiers and thieves,
Monks and whores, men of public trust, actors and clowns.
I must not think of you, whom God and I have damned—
It is enough my cloak remarks my daughter's hand.
She bears the contagion of your abandonment
As if it were a season on the fields, sunlight and dust,
Cloudbursts and cold, those things that do permit at last
Of harvests. Bertrande, the same shame encloses us.

I shall go now across the way. In the valley,
In the long reach of the snow, I shall lift up my head.
May you and Sanxi find me, small in the country,
And sign me back farewell. And I too shall disappear.

The Hotel 1829

For An Painter

Dusk—and the shimmer on the sea
has quickened and gone still. The large,
lithe hurricane birds soar in circles
beyond the bay, and filmy flamboyants
stand on the green embankment wavering.

A goat saunters in the street. Its eyes
gleam in the headlamps like amber
held up to the moon. Curious,
seeming not to see, they remain
in afterimages. She finds them
in the wine, the bright crystal
    at her place.

The glitter on the fog is rain;
the rainy reach, the long beach curves
out on the gloss, the vault of lights.
She sees oysters shining in their shells.
Her hand on the hard linen, in candlelight,
    expresses her.

In a reflected arc the goat's eyes,
in the goat's eyes a random will—and
the late, faint shimmer on the sea.

Great white ships roll in the harbor, illumined
and gracious to the night, their ornaments
burn on the blur beyond the Hotel 1829.

Concession

Believe the sullen sense that sickness made,
And broke you in its hands.

Believe that death inhabits the mere shade
Intimacy demands.

I drink, my love, to your profound disease;
Its was the better suit.

I could not have provided you this ease,
Nor this peace, absolute.

Woman Waiting on a Porch

Hot and slovenly,
You imagine moving
Towards a bleaker light,
An emptiness.

Go. The soft red morning
Touches strife to your blood.
You imagine
Quiet and ice,

Enough to close
Accounts too lately here,
A dipping of the moon
To the black, jagged range.

Mogollon Morning

The sun
From the sere south
Splays the ocotillo.
Cold withdraws. Still I stand among
Black winds.

The long,
Long bands of rock,
Old as wonder, stand back.
I listen for my death song there
In rock.

Old earth
In long shadows,
You pray my days to me.
I keep the ways of tortoises.
Keep me.

Prayer

Darkness,
You are forever.
   Aho.
You are before the light.
   Aho.
You stain the long ledge above the seep
      at Leaning Walls.
   Aho.
You are the smoke of silence burning.
   Aho.
Above, below, beyond, among the glittering things,
      you are.
   Aho.
The days descend in you,
     yesterday,
     today,
      the day to die.
   Aho.
   Aho.
   Aho.
   Aho.

Four Charms

1.

My child,
can you reach those berries,
the red and blue and purple berries?
They are delicious, perhaps.

2.

The bear is coming.
There are pitiful cries.
There are knives for mourning.

The bear is coming.
There are bones all about.
There are entrails on the ground.

The bear is coming.
Someone very old has said so.

3.

At the very sight of my horse,
at the very sight of my trappings,
at the very sight of my shield,
you are afraid, aren't you?

4.

The wind is cold,
isn't it?
The moon is dark,
isn't it?
The plain is wide,
isn't it?

Death dances at the base of that hill.

Rings of Bone

There were rings of bone
on the bandoliers of old men dancing.

Then, in the afternoon stippled with leaves
and the shadows of leaves,
the leaves glistened
and their shine shaped the air.

Now the leaves are dead.
Cold comes upon the leaves
and they are crisped upon the stony ground.
Webs of rime, like leaves, fasten on the mould,
and the wind divides and devours the leaves.

Again the leaves have more or less to do
with time. Music pervades the death of leaves.
The leaves clatter like the rings of bone
on the bandoliers of old men dancing.

Scaffold Bear

"Bears love the taste of whisky."
—Esther Nahgahnub, 1983

Here in this cave of sleep
I know of an animal on the slope;
No one has seen it,
But there are stories.
Juan Reyes dreamed of it too.
It reared against a moonlit cloud
And sundered the dream.
A young girl spoke of it with wonder,
Having heard it scoop the river for its food.

My own story is this:
A good man killed himself.
The next morning a bear, stripped of its hide,
Lay on a scaffold in a range of trees,
Bleeding, breathing faintly.
Its great paws had been removed.
The bear spoke to someone there, perhaps to me.
For in this cave of sleep,
I am at home to bears.

If It Could Ascend

I behold there
the far, faint motion of leaves.
The leaves shine,
and they will shiver down to death.
Something like a leaf lies here within me;
it wavers almost not at all,
and there is no light to see it by—
that it withers upon a black field.
If it could ascend the thousand years into my mouth,
I would make a word of it at last,
and I would speak it into the silence of the sun.

My Words Do Not Hold

For my father

My words do not hold,
for I am dead.
Nothing remains of me now—
nothing now.
I am not there in the range of time,
and my fine hands
do not make the signs
that meant my love,
that drew respect, that struck fear.

Do you hear?—
My breath ravels on the spool of winter.

Listen:
My words do not hold.
My face darkens in the awful turning,
and,
listening to the winds that wheel away,
you ask after me
and hear only the winds wheeling.

Carnegie, Oklahoma, 1919

This afternoon is older
than the giving of gifts
and the rhythmic scraping of the red earth.
My father's father's name is called,
and the gift horse stutters out, whole,
the whole horizon in its eyes.
In the giveaway is beaded
the blood memories of fathers and sons.
Oh, there is nothing like this afternoon
in all the miles and years around,
and I am not here,
but, grandfather, father, I am here.

Lawrence Ranch

Lawrence named it Kiowa.
The Lawrence Tree,
twisted density of black,
fronts the dawn,

stakes the silence
coyotes crack
as they stitch the field.
Light,

appearing barely
as a thinnest wash,
seeps from the ridge,
and day breaks

in successions of the sun
reporting westward
across the cold, kindled land
towards Tierra Amarilla.

December 29, 1890

Wounded Knee Creek

In the shine of photographs
are the slain, frozen and black

on a simple field of snow.
They image ceremony:

women and children dancing,
old men prancing, making fun.

In autumn there were songs, long
since muted in the blizzard.

In summer the wild buckwheat
shone like fox fur and quillwork,

and dusk guttered on the creek.
Now in serene attitudes

of dance, the dead in glossy
death are drawn in ancient light.

Fort Sill

Set-angia

You were riding in a wagon to the train.
A tree took shape in the distance.

You began to sing; it was more than unseemly.
The words of your song were so powerful
That nothing less than death could contain them.

At times, many years later, I hear the song,
Not as it was, but as it sounds across time.

Oh my warrior! I love you to sing!
The rattle of your breath, rising to the sun,
I hear among the screams of the hunting horses.

At Risk

I played at words.
It was a long season.

Soft syllables,
Images that shimmered,
Intricate etymologies.

They cohered in wonder.
I was enchanted.

My soul was at risk.
I struggled
Towards hurt,
Towards healing,
Towards passion,
Towards peace.

I wheeled in the shadow of a hawk.
Dizziness came upon me;
The turns of time confined and confounded me.

I lay in a cave,
On a floor cured in blood.

Ancient animals danced about me,
Presenting themselves formally,
In masks.

And there was I, among ancient animals,
In the formality of the dance,
Remembering my face in the mirror of masks.

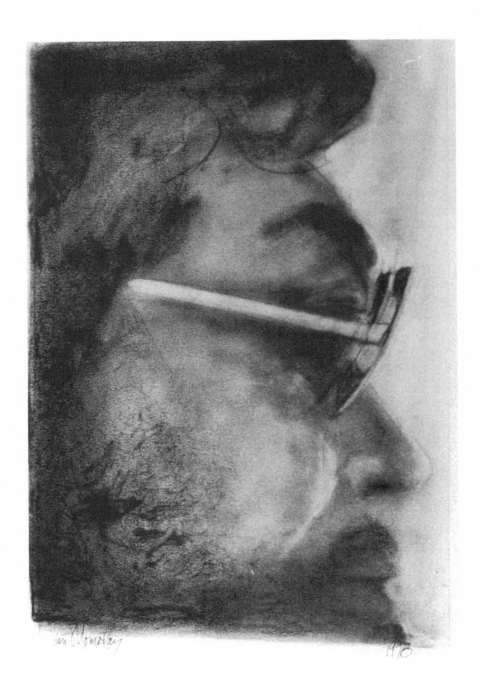

About the Author

N. Scott Momaday is a poet, novelist, painter, playwright, and storyteller. He resides in the American Southwest, and he is Regents Professor of the Humanities at the University of Arizona. Among his numerous awards are the Academy of American Poets Prize, the Pulitzer Prize, and the Premio Letterario Internazionale "Mondello." He is a member of the Kiowa Gourd Dance Society and a Fellow of the American Academy of Arts and Sciences. He walks long distances, and he rides an Appaloosa mare named "Ma'am." At his best he cooks. He is justly famous for a recipe named "The Washita Crossing Soup," the ingredients of which are, in his words, "simple, sacred, and secret." He is a bear.